SandCastle

Rhyme Time

Eli and the High Pie

Anders Hanson

Consulting Editor, Diane Craig, M.A./Reading Specialist

ABDO
Publishing Company

Published by ABDO Publishing Company, 4940 Viking Drive, Edina, Minnesota 55435.

Printed in the United States.

Credits
Edited by: Pam Price
Curriculum Coordinator: Nancy Tuminelly
Cover and Interior Design and Production: Mighty Media
Photo Credits: BananaStock Ltd., Brand X Pictures, Digital Vision, Kelly Doudna, Eyewire Images, Francis Hammond/PhotoAlto, Hemera, PhotoDisc, Stockbyte

Library of Congress Cataloging-in-Publication Data

Hanson, Anders, 1980-
    Eli and the high pie / Anders Hanson.
        p. cm. -- (Rhyme time)
    Includes index.
    ISBN 1-59197-789-4 (hardcover)
    ISBN 1-59197-895-5 (paperback)
    1. English language--Rhyme--Juvenile literature. I. Title. II. Rhyme time (ABDO Publishing Company)

PE1517.H375 2004
428.1'3--dc22
                                                                              2004049512

SandCastle™ books are created by a professional team of educators, reading specialists, and content developers around five essential components that include phonemic awareness, phonics, vocabulary, text comprehension, and fluency. All books are written, reviewed, and leveled for guided reading, early intervention reading, and Accelerated Reader® programs and designed for use in shared, guided, and independent reading and writing activities to support a balanced approach to literacy instruction.

Let Us Know

After reading the book, SandCastle would like you to tell us your stories about reading. What is your favorite page? Was there something hard that you needed help with? Share the ups and downs of learning to read. We want to hear from you! To get posted on the ABDO Publishing Company Web site, send us e-mail at:

sandcastle@abdopub.com

SandCastle Level: Transitional

Words that rhyme do not have to be spelled the same. These words rhyme with each other:

by

sigh

fry

sky

high

sty

lie

pie

tie

try

The crowd watches the parade go **by**.

Betsy is at the top of the slide.

It is very **high**.

Alexander is about to eat a french fry.

Samuel always tells his dad
the truth.

He doesn't **lie**.

Jess holds on to the balloons so they won't float up into the **sky**.

Timothy and his dad are baking an apple pie.

Two piglets are in the mud in their sty.

Cathy is bored.

She puts her head down with a big sigh.

Katherine doesn't know if she will get a hit, but she is going to try.

Lucas dressed up for the party.

He is wearing a yellow shirt and a blue tie.

Eli and the High Pie

Eli's mom is baking a pie.
Mom truly loves her son, Eli.
He's the apple of her eye.

But Eli does not feel
like the apple of Mom's eye
when she puts the pie way up high.

Eli wondered why
Mom put the pie
so high.

"Your room
smells like a sty,"
Mom said with a sigh.
"Until it is clean,
there will be no pie."

18

Eli wants that pie so much he could cry.

But the mess in his room is sky high.

That he could not deny.

19

It was so much work
he thought he would cry.
"I could be here until next July!"
But he knew that he would have to try.

20

He called to his mom, who was nearby.
"Hey, Mom, my room is no longer a sty.
Now may I have my favorite pie?"

Rhyming Riddle

What do you call a pigpen that is up in a tree?

High sty

Glossary

parade. a public procession held in celebration

piglet. a baby pig

pigpen. a fenced area where pigs are kept; a dirty place

sigh. a loud breath that expresses a feeling such as relief, frustration, or sadness

sty. a pigpen

About SandCastle™

A professional team of educators, reading specialists, and content developers created the SandCastle™ series to support young readers as they develop reading skills and strategies and increase their general knowledge. The SandCastle™ series has four levels that correspond to early literacy development in young children. The levels are provided to help teachers and parents select the appropriate books for young readers.

Emerging Readers
(no flags)

Beginning Readers
(1 flag)

Transitional Readers
(2 flags)

Fluent Readers
(3 flags)

These levels are meant only as a guide. All levels are subject to change.

To see a complete list of SandCastle™ books and other nonfiction titles from ABDO Publishing Company, visit www.abdopub.com or contact us at: 4940 Viking Drive, Edina, Minnesota 55435 • 1-800-800-1312 • fax: 1-952-831-1632